Bet

Hi Mom! Hi Dad!

101 cartoons for
New Parents
by Lynn Johnston

MEADOWBROOK PRESS
18318 Minnetonka Blvd.
Deephaven, Minnesota 55391

Meadowbrook Press Edition

SEVENTH PRINTING January 1981

PRINTED IN THE UNITED STATES OF AMERICA
Library of Congress Number 77-82216
ISBN 0-915658-06-2

Published by Meadowbrook Press, Inc.
18318 Minnetonka Blvd. Deephaven, MN 55391

THE FIRST YEAR OF LIFE

A tiny bundle of life is placed in your arms, and at first it's hard to believe that you are now a parent. The overwhelming feeling of responsibility for another life, the pride and joy in your "creation", but also the concomitant feelings of inadequacy in your new role, frequently surface during that first year.

Lynn Johnston, with humour and sensitivity, creates cartoons that depict the feelings and reactions of parents as they learn to respond to the needs of the growing child, to the reactions of in-laws and relatives, to the pressures of the mass media, the experts, and the child-rearing fads. As we chuckle at the captions, we are reminded of the incredible amount of hardship experienced by parents during the baby's first year—the loss of sleep, the feeling of helplessness when the baby cries and can't be comforted, and the new precautions we have to take as the baby acquires new competencies and skills, as he or she learns to reach and grasp objects, sit up, creep, and finally becomes upright and mobile.

The baby becomes a "real" personality and enriches the life of the family. The joy experienced by the parents makes the struggle well worthwhile. The recognition of this joy is captured in the last cartoon: "To think that before we had a baby, this was just the same old park!"

With a few deft strokes of her pen, Lynn Johnston shows us what the first year of life is like. Her delightfully subtle cartoons at once make the hardships of life with baby more bearable.

— Mary Blum, Psychologist

7

8

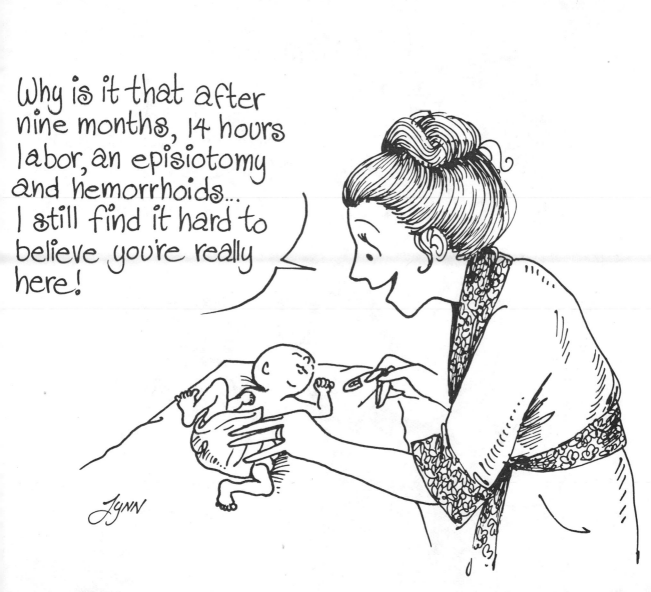

9

13

14

15

16

17

18

19

I haven't seen myself without hair there since I was twelve....
LYNN

24

30

35

37

I've tried feeding and rocking...and singing...and burping and bathing and pleading...and walking and shouting and whispering and...changing...and....

Dear Mom, you ask if we enjoy parenthood. Well, after 3 weeks of getting used to the situation, I can safely say ~~that we are already~~ that ~~things are~~ ~~that the baby is~~ Mom, can you make it out here?

LYNN

42

43

44

Ooh, what's this ucky stuff mummy's putting in my mouf? Not so fast mummy, we want to learn to swallow, don't we. Ooh! needs to be a little cooler. Don't burn my wittle lipsies.... Watch it, mummy, don't you know how to feed baby?...
LYNN

49

50

53

54

58

60

61

I know what you're going through, Donnie.. When my little sister was born, I lost all interest in sports & science — took up squeaky toys, talked gibberish, & demanded late night feedings.

71

74

75

83

84

85

95

98

101

It's nice to be needed.

FREE STUFF BOOKS

FREE STUFF FOR PARENTS

Over 250 of the best free and up-to-a-dollar booklets and samples parents can get by mail:
- sample teethers
- booklets on pregnancy & childbirth
- sample newsletters

$3.45 ppd.

FREE STUFF FOR KIDS

Over 250 of the best free and up-to-a-dollar things kids can get by mail:
- coins & stamps
- bumper stickers & decals
- posters & maps

$3.45 ppd.

FREE STUFF FOR COOKS

Over 250 of the best free and up-to-a-dollar booklets and samples cooks can get by mail:
- cookbooks & recipe cards
- money-saving shopping guides
- seeds & spices

$3.45 ppd.

LYNN JOHNSTON BOOKS
Creator of "For Better or For Worse"

DAVID, WE'RE PREGNANT!

101 laughing-out-loud cartoons by Lynn Johnston that accentuate the humorous side of conceiving, expecting and giving birth.

$3.45 ppd.

HI MOM! HI DAD!

101 cartoons about all the funny things that happen after you get your baby home, during the first twelve months of parenthood.

$3.45 ppd.

DO THEY EVER GROW UP?

A hilarious, 101-cartoon survival guide for parents of the tantrum and pacifier set—all about the terrible two's and the pre-school years.

$3.45 ppd.

WATCH ME GROW

The #1 selling baby memory and record book to cover baby's first five years. Illustrated by Lynn Johnston

Hardcover. $9.00 ppd.

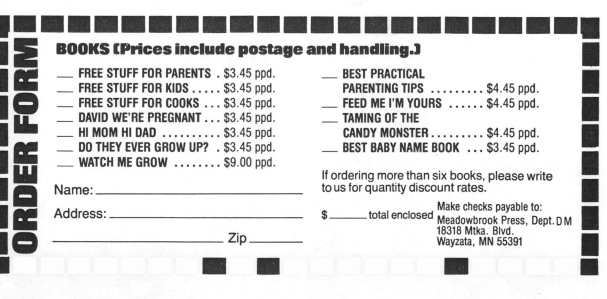